Choking back the DEVIL

Published by Raw Dog Screaming Press
Bowie, MD
All rights reserved.
First Edition

Cover: Steven Archer
Book design: Jennifer Barnes
Printed in the United States of America
ISBN: 978-1-947879-12-6

Library of Congress Control Number: 2019942338

www.RawDogScreaming.com

Choking back the DEVIL

Poetry by
Donna Lynch

RAW DOG
SCREAMING
PRESS

Contents

Foreword

Donna Lynch brings no baggage to her poetry. In the street punk witch *chic* of *Choking Back the Devil* there is no room for baggage. The burdens of existence described by Lynch carry such weight that the reader cannot take on another ounce of emotion. This is not the high society of Edith Wharton or the noir opulence of the Bronte sisters. Lynch's words come from the asphalt of pain that belongs to the contemporary woman who finds no shelter under the porticos of Facebook platitudes of everything being wonderful and special posted by those who claim a dull, effortless life.

Lynch has moved beyond any cliche of genre you may find populating speculative poetry to claim her street corner and her flickering lamp. She is the shadow in the light that you see peripherally as you try to walk home at night hoping you are safe from harm. Lynch reminds you that you are not safe, sometimes not even from yourself.

Choking Back the Devil leads us to the cutting line between horror and mental illness. Is it the soul at stake or the mind? Perhaps there is no difference. Is this horror or a journey of mental collapse? Are the witches, demons and monsters she describes real or imaginings born of a broken psyche? The reader must decide the path to be followed and the collateral damage resulting from either choice.

The book begins with an anthem called *Legend* proclaiming *Take every bit of pain they gave you/… and build your demon/ your urban legend.* Pain is life and life is pain she is telling us. Pain is what molds you and you need to embrace it to become the demon you most fear. When we think of personal demons, addictions and self-destruction come to mind. Such is sometimes the cycle of mental illness. But demons are powerful creatures as well. And if pain is what makes you powerful Lynch tells her readers to grow strong with it. Yet Lynch recognizes the horrible paradox of this struggle. Sometimes you join the dark, sometimes the dark consumes you. In the title poem she writes *You cannot know/… What it is to be consumed/ By something so inviting.*

The idea of the temptation from an invitation to destruction and the struggle between merging with darkness and being consumed by it highlights many of her pieces. It brings to mind Joseph Conrad's famous "fascination with the abomination" allusions in *Heart of Darkness*. Lynch's narrators are all drawn to mental suffering much as a co-dependent might; almost as if addicted to suffering. But as Lynch will tell you in *You, Alone* we are Mr. Kurtz; we chose to take that boat traveling beyond chartered territory: *The most terrifying thing/is when you come to understand/ There is no curse upon your bloodline/…you alone are responsible/for the damages incurred.* Yet even this recognition can bring no comfort. You may well know you are on the road to mental ruin but something about this kind of illness draws you further and further beyond hope.

This core theme resonates throughout her volume. It is up to us to be consumed or to grow strong from it if we are lucky enough to break free. Lynch offers no easy solutions only the truism that pain will be your companion in this journey.

It is cliché to try to corral the term "dark poetry" as if it is nothing more than the musings of the malcontent. Dark verse has been the staple of poetry since Homer's *Iliad*. You can find examples in poets we all have come to know, often for more gentile subjects, such as Robert Frost's *Witch of Coos*, Coleridge's *The Rime of the Ancient Mariner*, Wallace Stevens' eerie *Domination of Black*. Even Dylan Thomas' sad nostalgic *Fern Hill* ends with death as paramount over youth. Dark poetry is the red wine of horror; dry, robust and full of tannin.

Lynch's *Choking Back the Devil* is a luscious vintage indeed. Lynch blends the modern with the ancient. In *The Horse, the Home* Lynch describes what could be a possession or something even deeper involving a woman facing a change in life through sex and death—"So it climbed inside of me/ and I did not resist." In that poem you see a hint of Celtic mythology. The Black Horse in Celtic myths represented both death and dark forces as well as a messenger of esoteric knowledge. The Celtic Black Horse was a keeper of secrets and mysteries. Here too the narrator adopts this interloper of her sex and life and becomes part of the keeper of the secret and mysterious; finding solace in this knowledge—*I am more than a thing that it haunts /I am more than a horse that it rides/ I am its home/...and there's nothing quite like the feeling of being held from the inside.*

This rich mixture of the allegorical, metaphorical and metaphysical gives us something more than just dark verse.

There is a street-wise wisdom here. Lynch has lived this pain and like the ancient mariner stops us to tell this story.

I find something transformative in this work. Something far beyond the typical presentation of archetypes we often see in speculative poetry. I think this volume elevates Lynch to the next tier of upcoming dark poets that will dominate the genre.

David E. Cowen

Bram Stoker Nominated Poet for *Bleeding Safron*

Introduction

Demons come in many forms
Some with teeth and some with horns
But none so vicious as the hordes
That came to be when you were born.

Legend

Take every bit of pain they gave you

All the shame you feel

All the damage you ask for

And every bit you didn't

and build your demon

your urban legend

Because those painful things aren't pieces of you they've taken

They are gifts given

And they will make you famous

if you let them

Turn to cemetery stone

Let them spend the night in your arms

On a bet or a dare

And steal their lives by morning

Wait by the old bridge

on that road in the back-country

Let them hear you sharpening your ax on the river rocks
as they idle

Name yourself
Let them call you from the mirror
in the dark
Let them set you free
Then rip them apart

They will make you famous
if you let them.

Committed to Memory

The night I was committed is lost from my memory
I know I went, but don't know why
I'm sure someone could tell me
But I don't want to know

It won't be something grand
some mad spectacle
I know it's something weak and shameful
A diorama I only put together the night before
incomplete
poorly constructed
And I remember the humiliation from way back then
That's all I need to know

The only thing that haunts me
The only piece I can't escape
(and it's the piece I'll always be expecting)
is that if I can't recall that ugly winter night
What else have I forgotten?

Choking Back the Devil

All the Things They Never Tell You

When Witches get trapped in hallway mirrors
and those mirrors break
It just makes more witches

The Devil doesn't possess children
He just takes the blame
So no one has to face the fact that
some children are broken for no reason

Angels walk among us
but they are not love, they are not here to help
Not a single one

When people die
They feel like cold, heavy meat
Even the ones you love

No one will ever notice you
as much as those who wish to see you suffer

Donna Lynch

those who wish to see you fail
And those people will notice everything

Every single thing you do
is a desperate attempt to evade fear
deep down inside

Your body will betray you
Your brain will betray you worse
but will lie and tell you otherwise

And one day you will lose everything you love
which is the most terrifying
Of all the things they never tell you.

Terror Management Theory

You know that feeling

That rush of hot chemicals that floods your body

When you suddenly remember

That you didn't exist for eons

And there will come a time when you won't exist again?

That's just your brain pissing itself in fear.

Carry on.

Race

Horror, they say, shouldn't hurt women or children or animals

The villain shouldn't win

The protagonist shouldn't die

It should take you to the edge but never throw you over

There should always be a reason for the torture

But that isn't horror

What they want is an escape from the storm on the horizon

Barreling its way toward them

Like it does for all of us

They want a story that acknowledges their fear

but doesn't cross that final finish line

It doesn't reach the event horizon

It doesn't break the rules

But that isn't horror

We don't mean real life horror, they say

But that's all there is

Choking Back the Devil

Everyone is a villain in someone's story

And everyone is afraid to see the finish line ahead.

You, Alone

The most terrifying thing
is when you come to understand
that you are not haunted
there is no demon in you
and monsters are not real
There is no catastrophic storm inside your heart
no ancient war being fought with your bones
There is no curse upon your bloodline
no debt that must be paid
no Devil's trick
But that you are only you
and you alone are responsible
for the damages incurred.

The Horse, the Home

I wasn't so receptive in the beginning
I hadn't even been looking
or put out an invitation
I don't remember calling
but it found me
it chose me

When it began to follow me
I quickened my pace
but everywhere I went
it went with me
one step closer
every time
the slow build
becoming more familiar
with each passing day
until I would turn and look for it
making sure it was still there

and if I couldn't feel it
I would walk faster
cat and mouse
voluntary prey

When it began to ride me
it was too much
but a heavy relief
because now I knew for sure that it was there
its unnatural limbs
all sinew and pulses
gripping tightly as I moved
affecting my gait by force and
restriction

don't fall off
I'd think
don't fall off
I'd grasp for it
but there was nothing for my hands to hold
and my heart ached at the loss

So it climbed inside of me
and I did not resist

even as it strained through my pores in a billion tiny threads
coiling like nerves
like a mass of silken tendrils
reassembling on the inside of my skin

I did not cry as it permeated my muscles
with a pressure I could never imagine
like a heavy blade on anesthetized tissue

I did not flinch as it crashed through my bones
like a beast
all hoof and horn
barreling through a dense grove
the tattered carnage of hide and tendon swinging from its antlers

And I did not protest as it filled up my organs
devouring the material and mass
drinking in the fluids
until there was nothing left of me

I am more than a thing that it haunts
I am more than a horse that it rides
I am its home
and I know the things it's seen

I know the darkness and dream-like void it inhabited before me

the terror and calm of a world without time

but I am not afraid

because I am not alone

and there's nothing quite like the feeling of being held from
the inside.

Wreckage

It was never me getting in
and wrecking the place
until you had to evict me

It was always me letting you in
and keeping you there
held hostage among the wreckage
until you felt there was no better home.

If You Love Me

If you love me
it will feel like the time you stood on a bridge
and though you were not suicidal
you still thought you might jump

or the time
you were bathing the baby
and though you are not a monster
thought: what if I let her slip under

If you love me
it will feel like the time you were shaving
and though you did not want to bleed
imagined gouging the blade into your neck

For if you love me
if you let me inside
I will make you doubt your every move

Choking Back the Devil

but instead of distrusting me
you'll only distrust yourself.

My Incomplete Children

They've all been so different

They look like words and stories with no endings
undeveloped.

They look like dreams who aged with me
pale and unfulfilled

They are just masses of tissue, masses of me, growing in the
    wrong place
incomplete and never meant to thrive

But as I reach the halfway point
As I move closer to the void
I know I have to push my babies from their nest
into the world
ready or not
And the only comfort that I have is knowing
that they all have teeth.

Sacrifice

We hear the witch come in
Shuffling and scraping
But by the time we do
It's often too late

At least for some of us

We are too many
with too few places to hide

It's always a small foot slipped from beneath a bed
or a lock of hair spilling from behind the cupboard door
that last little body that couldn't quite fit

That's the one who goes

We do not know what she does with us
Maybe our insides get eaten
Maybe our hair and teeth become decorations and talismans

Donna Lynch 29

Maybe our bones are used to etch symbols on doors of
    homes, cursing those inside
We do not know
For we are not witches
but discarded children who once believed that fairytales
    about witches were
folly
and horror only came from starvation and shadowy men on
    the streets

But we know better now

Then one night
After the smallest and sweetest among us was taken
Someone remembered a fable about mice
And a cat

The cat was taking them one by one at night
But
If they put a bell about his neck
They'd hear him coming sooner
They'd have more time to hide

It was a grand idea

everyone agreed
But begged the question

Who would bell the cat?

So we bit our lips and glanced around and it was decided
that the oldest among us
should choose who would bell the witch

I am the oldest
I am the one who will make the decision
I am the one who will send a trembling child into her
    terrible mouth
to save the rest
Just as I am the one who gathers the children
every time the witch comes

I do my best to hide them all
But I know there will always be the one
who doesn't fit
And as I gather them
I know which one it will have to be
I am the one who chooses

And so I look among these tiny faces
Their eyes brimming with tears and nightmares
I make my decision
and silently wonder who it is that will someday
need to bell me.

Choking Back the Devil

Queens

You ask how Queens become so evil
Screaming for heads and organs ad nauseum
Maybe it's simple:
They are missing vital pieces
They are filled with empty spaces
(and you *can* be filled with nothing)
They pack the holes with rotting fruit
excised pig hearts, severed limbs, and lengths of silken thread
But never anything that fits
Never anything that works
Never anything that heals the wounds
Or makes the crowns less heavy on their regal, weary heads

But I am not a queen
Mostly witch, sometimes bard
So this is speculation and maybe I'm all wrong
When I'm done pulling out the blood-encrusted gauze
    from my own black cavities that never seem to heal
And when I'm done replacing it with a fresh and healthy

Donna Lynch   33

mass of validation

A sterile mesh made of desire and adoration

And my gaping wounds are impacted with soft, absorbent
webs of empty promises

to never lie to never hurt to never leave

I'll ponder it some more and try to imagine why we—these
queens and fools—do this to ourselves.

She's a Dream

To the bored and the desperate
The empty and dry
Just whisper the words:
You're a dream

She's not like the others
She's witty and wry
She cusses and drinks
She's a dream

She says all the right things
And tears down your walls
And hides when she's told
She's a dream

She brings you to life
She's a really good time
(Save that time that she cried)
Still a dream

Donna Lynch   35

But last week at the bar
When your wife called you home
And you left her alone
What a scene

It was good for a while
Now she's calling your house
When the hours are late
Can't she see

There's too much at risk
Your job and your kids
She misunderstands
What you need

We were just having fun
And blowing off steam
Our plans were not real
They were dreams

But she's ripped out her hair
And followed you home
And waits in dark
In the reeds

Choking Back the Devil

And when the sun rises
(If you make it that long)
All you'll have are regrets
And your pleas

To the bored and the desperate
The empty and dry
Shut your mouth, bite your tongue
And take heed

Don't breathe her to life
And make her feel real
Just to blink her away
In your sleep

The price is too high
And the causalities, many
From a nightmare mistook
For a dream.

Succubi

We try to tell them they don't want it

But they never believe

So we open our mouths and our legs

and let them in

Then we open their throats and their chest cavities

and let ourselves in

It's thirsty work

but fortunately, the fluids are plentiful.

Choking Back the Devil

The Loss of Gods

The gods, the ghosts, the fates
packed up and left one day in May
I waited like a child on Christmas Eve
I waited like I used to on my birthday
For Santa
For my father
And like them both
The spirits never came

A friend, one day, told me he didn't know if he believed in god
but it was a prettier story if he did
It was the truest thing I ever heard

It should've made things simpler
But life weighs heavier now
There is a fear, deeper than fear
A terror that we all encounter
But there's no lovely mask on mine
Nothing to cover its unmerciful, empty face

Donna Lynch

So if the gods have shielded you

or wrapped their shimmering veils and robes around you

to protect you from the Void

Pray they never leave you naked

Pray they never leave you.

The Cult of Immolaine

Amid the secret, waking nightmares she endured
we found each other
A deep cold hell that pooled around her
Mine was more a storm inside me
Our ugly humor keeping us from drowning
She was so scared of drowning

We talked of mutilation
Psycho killers and their demons
And we laughed to show them we were unafraid
We lit candles on altars
Praying to a saint we had created
We carried hammers just in case she didn't come
But she must come

She will set the shore ablaze
To dry us to our bones and keep us warm
Saint Immolaine would never let us drown
Until the night she did

The demons swam around us in the pool

Coming in like sharks

every time she bled

Gasping for her breath she cried for Immolaine

We did not pray enough

She cried to me

We did not believe enough

She cried to god

But I knew how to swim

A faster minnow than my sister

I knew to drop the hammer

so that I might float

I knew not to thrash and flail

revealing all my injuries

I did not bleed and lead them to me

We pulled her from the pool

From the mouths of apex predators

Immolaine and I

And our blessed saint told her what to do

So she'd never have to drown again

So she'd never be devoured underwater

And with that sacred knowledge

She stood tall upon the shores of hell
And set her pretty self on fire.

The Most Haunted Girl I Ever Knew

The most haunted girl I ever knew
Her name has since been <redacted>
In case she ever reads this
and in case she doesn't remember
In case she doesn't know

She shivered and cried at everything
the dark
at music
at the sky
and the rain
screaming for a reason we could not know
at trees and creeks and roads
always spinning
breathlessly
trying to free herself from the unbreakable webs of wraiths
always spinning
choking on nothing but air
that she might unchain herself from her own body

stumbling into briers
and screaming louder at the tiny drops of blood

We didn't know it then
It was better to think that she'd invented too many wild friends
It was better to think that it was ghosts
That the haunted hands that touched her came from
    beyond the veil
rather than from beneath her blankets
We didn't know it then

I wish we'd known it then.

Treat

I'm hungry for something small
said the Wendigo
as he changed into a man
and stepped up into
the empty ice cream truck.

Guest

I didn't buy the statue
It's the wrong style for my house
It's proportions are off
If I were to buy a statue
it would be life-size
or mere inches
Not this terrible in-between height
Like a stone toddler

And it's ugly

It showed up one day at my door
I was going to leave it out there
or put it far away in the woods
but a sense of dread kept me from touching it
as though I knew it would try to touch me back

It's *so* ugly

I didn't bring it in
I *never* would've brought it in
but here it is
in the hallway
and I hate it
and it hates me
Of this
I am certain

I haven't had anyone over since it arrived
I can't
Everyone asks and I tell them the truth
Where did it come from?
They ask
What does it look like?
But I don't know the answer to the first question
and I can't tell them the second

If I tell them
If I describe it
I know things won't be the same for them

They don't understand and neither do I
but I know I can't say it

Yet they push and push
They've come over unannounced
hoping I'd let them in
peering around me
trying to see it
and they don't understand that I'm trying to protect them
I'm trying to keep everything from changing
but still they push
they are worried, they say
because I don't leave the house now
I don't eat
and my hair is matted and greasy
my clothes stink like yeast
so they push because they are worried, they say

but I think they push because they can't stand not knowing

and lately

I'm ready to say it
I'm so close

It's coming closer, too
It moves so slowly

you can barely tell

but it moves

closer to the door

and it's only a matter of time

before I say it

before I tell them

and it will be on its way

to them

to you.

Choking Back the Devil

Visitors

Never asleep
Always dreaming
Is exactly how they want you

The Static Men, The Silver-Nail Woman, The Smothering Body,
And The Biting Cat

Eyes open
Never moving
This is exactly how they want you

They will touch you.

Woman

I hate the woman who stands at the edge of my woods
For many reasons
Not the least being that she doesn't really stand
She hangs
not by a rope
not by her neck
but like a tree limb, heavy with water, battered down by rain
no shoes on her muddy feet
There's nothing in her dirty hands
and nothing in her hollow eyes but thick, wet strands of
    matted hair
Her skin is broken
I can see the cuts and bites from here
As though animals attack her every night
her clothes are barely there
she doesn't speak
she doesn't cry
she just gazes at my house
every night

until the dawn

when she turns and walks back into the trees

Once I tried to give her a story

A narrative to make me less afraid

Maybe she's looking for help

Held captive and tortured as her wounds would imply

Even if she were a ghost

I would be less afraid

But no history fits her

Something won't let it

Something inside eats the words

Which is why

I hate the woman who stands at the edge of my woods

But I'll hate her more

when she knocks on my door.

Everything You Love

I waited what I felt was an appropriate amount of time for
    her ghost
I knew she would find her way back home
But maybe she wouldn't come back to me because I let her go
I had to let her go

Maybe it was the concussion I got the next day
Maybe it closed a gate
Maybe it shattered the piece of me inside my skull that believed
When I hit my head
And my stomach turned to poison
And everything went black

Maybe I slipped into the void
Because I think I live there now

But not with her

I moved into her house

in case she changed her mind
I kept her ring on my finger
so she could see the light reflecting
I watched so hard
Then I stopped watching
because that's the wiser thing to do

Maybe I can only know the void
Because I think it lives here now

But not with her

You will someday lose everything you love
but nothing so quick as your belief
that the things you love will come back.

Hunger

I ate your hands that I might have your strength
Your mouth, that I might finally speak
Your heart to steal your bravery
I'll eat the rest once you're asleep.

Choking Back the Devil

I am choking back the devil
with every kiss and every cry
I will have to swallow harder
until my mouth is dry

He made his home inside me
I no longer wonder why
He slipped in slowly, deeply
Hollowed me completely
With no regret or mercy
No deception nor disguise

When I'm pushing he is pulling
When I'm silent he is speaking
When I'm screaming
he is clawing at my throat

He guides my hands
and moves my tongue

Until the thirsty work is done
And the cities are on fire
and the exits are all locked

You cannot know
You cannot know
I cry
What it is to be consumed
By something so inviting
That will bite until you're gone

So I am choking back the devil
And it tastes of blood and brine
I will have to swallow harder
Until my mouth is dry.

You Knew

I'm the serpent in the story
That bites the trusting hand
But I offer them no sorrow
They know exactly who I am.

Cry

It isn't that I feel nothing
on the contrary
I feel everything
too deeply
too often
But my compassion drifts past the satellites in my skin
they transmit it with a sadness brimming in their cells
It glides too close to the void inside my torso
and approaches the event horizon just beneath my ribs
and is gone

You look at me
the way you look at the cold, black sky
terrified and small
and you need a sign
you need to know god can hear you
that I can hear you
anything that tells you I can feel the pain between us
the fear that I will rip you apart (because I will)

you beg for empathy
but I am empty now
and I wanted nothing more
than to open up to you and show you
every word of love, every tear of sorrow, that heavy crown
of guilt I ought to wear
and a fragile shroud of mercy I could wrap you in
but there is nothing here
I am naked and unmoved
and only one of us will feel it
only one of us will cry.

You Are Not You

You are not you

I said

As I gazed in the mirror, scissors in hand, and stripped down

Even though I wasn't wearing any clothes.

Body

I never had a perfect body

Not even a good one

All the starving

All the force-feeding and the purging

Then there were the strange hands on me

And stranger, sticky mouths

I called them by name but knew not one of them

The pills and the powders

and late nights turned to scorching sun

Walking home on burning sidewalks

The anxiety and abuse

I'm never comfortable

I'm never at home

I'm entirely ineffective

And I'm wishing I listened

When the other demons said to stop possessing broken
    young women

But I've never been great

At taking advice.

Donna Lynch   63

It Just Wasn't Your Night

It wasn't your face or your hair

or your legs

It wasn't that you reminded me of anyone

Not my mother

Not a lover or sister

It wasn't that you ever spurned me

nor the way that you carelessly let your cigarette burn down

all the way into crumbling ashes and embers

It wasn't any small detail

or anything tangible

It wasn't a look you gave me

or anyone

It wasn't the phase of the moon

or a terrible voice

You were just there

When the gnawing inside me turned into vicious biting

When the switch flipped and all my lights went out

When I had no choice but to seize the moment

You were there

You were there and it just wasn't your night.

Doll

I let the madmen practice on me
How far can I stretch
How deep do I go
How well do I hold under certain conditions

I let them work out their raw energies
Their mothers
Their preachers
Their sex and frustration

I can't curse or complain
My mouth is sewn shut
Filled with rags
And the hair of the girls they once loved

I can't see what comes next
I'm blinded and bound
Branded and broken
Skinned and de-gloved

Choking Back the Devil

Sometimes they cry
And sometimes they come
They see just how much
they can tighten the belts

They dress me in pearls
From dead grandmothers' necks
I'm both victim and muse
And I'm glad I can help

Honey

The youngest sister was the best at catching their eyes.

The middle sister was the best at the sell.

And the eldest sisters,

they took care of the rest.

This would be the way.

There were two things they needed in the ravaged land:

Food and shelter.

The former was in low supply.

The latter, expensive to keep.

Throughout the land, this was the way.

Their great-great-great grandparents had been orphaned together

Maybe by illness, maybe by war.

They would've died for sure

had the wolves not taken them in.

A funny thing, to be sure, but the wolves there were a

    different breed,

and this was their way.

As the generations went,
and as genetics go,
by the time the sisters were born
they didn't look much like wolves at all.
But they were.
Time does what it will
and that is always the way.

The sisters had heard the stories
and seen with their own eyes
the terrible things that man could do,
the terrible things he'd done to their wilderness
their kin
the people of the land
and they could not believe with their hopeful hearts that
this would have to be the way.
But it might always be the way.

Maybe they could bring some joy to the people of the land,
they agreed.
The people had so little joy.
Something lovely, something bright
Something sweet.

Everyone could enjoy something sweet now and then.
Wasn't that always the way?

So while man raped and killed
and destroyed the land,
while man murdered babies in front of their mothers
and shot the fathers in the head
and rolled the bodies into muddy ditches,
the sisters did the best they could to bring some joy
with what they had,
which was their parent's way.
It would be their way, too.

They rebuilt the hives and nursed the bees back to health.
It wasn't perfect,
they needed better and
they all struggled
but slowly, they began to thrive,
as is sometimes the way.

They collected the honey
and gave it to the poor
and the children were sticky and delighted
while the parents felt tiny, crystalline sparks in their hearts.

But they *sold* the honey to the men who came through in trucks
and machines.
The kind of men who never felt sparks in their hearts.
It just wasn't their way.

The youngest sister caught their eyes
at the roadside stand,
and they halted their trucks and machines
and looked at the jars with hungry gazes
and looked at the sister, hungrier still,
hoping for all things sweet.
The middle sister negotiated with them,
hinting at what they could have if they bought the honey,
she'd say, with a wink,
and the men thought,
well, with these kinds of girls,
this is usually the way.

So the men would pay the middle sister
and follow the youngest sister into the woods
where they were met with the eldest sisters
and their teeth
and their claws
and their hunger and rage.

Their trucks and machines were destroyed,
rolled into muddy ditches,
and the sisters fed
until the men were hollow shells,
as was a wolf's way.

And the viscous, bloody shells, it was discovered
were the perfect additions to the apiary,
just the right temperature for the bees,
just the right size.
So in the space that cold hearts
and stomachs
and lungs
and entrails once filled
there were only bees
working and thriving like they never had.
From then on, the honey was the best the people ever tasted,
the sisters kept their home safe and warm
and their bellies full,
and though no one ever spoke of glimpses of carnage
strewn through the evergreens,
and the growing pits of metal,
everyone in the land knew
this was the best

Choking Back the Devil

and the only
possible way.

I Try to Imagine Them Speaking

He suspended them
(What was left of them)
For our curiosity and
Almost pornographic education
So we could see
In a way we're never really allowed
But still
They do not look real
They do not look like us
So I gaze until I lose focus
Try to see them with skin
Try to see them with lights in their eyes
How their faces seem foreign
And I stare at their flaccid, useless tongues
And I try to imagine them speaking.

Excerpt From Skinned (1999)

BIRTH

At birth
I was little more than a serpent
A parasite and blind
Slick with oil and smashed
Ready to scream and tear through the envelope.

RUST

When I was a child I had a little house up the hill from the goat.
The serpent lived there in the wall, next to the shed.
I let him be as he stayed quiet.
We would track mud and dirt into the little house and
the spiders took up housekeeping in the summer.

Donna Lynch   75

Mice fed the snake when it snowed
and spring would bring the rains that brought the rust.
By fall, I'd have a full house to entertain.

By the time the goat had died
the layers of dirt were thick.
They laid him outside my door under a sheet and
called for a truck.
I caught the death shivers for the first time.

I brushed the dirt and leaves off of his sheet while we waited.
I've been cleaning up the dirt ever since.

The truck had the words "Valley Protein" written on the side.
 I was seventeen before I knew what it was.

THREE, NO...FOUR DEAD MEN

My former stepfather died at Christmas of kidney failure,
     I believe.
I had not seen him since I was sixteen.
His father was the warden of the State Penitentiary.

In my stepfather's dresser drawer there was an old black
    and white photograph
of three black inmates hanging from the gallows in the courtyard.
He just kept it there.
He never said why.
He liked me when I was ten.
When I turned thirteen he taught me about hate.
I pitied him, but didn't truly hate him until the day he
made my grandmother cry.
He was 6'7" tall and probably close to 300 lbs.
Now he is a small pile of ash.
I don't know what became of the photograph.

PAPER

There are layers of paper beyond my skin that I keep
    pictures and words
in specific order on.
This is how I know and remember where things belong.
If you were to peel off my skin
it would be as hieroglyphics etched on muscle.
Cell memory.

And beyond that, well...it's chaos.
My rooms are neat and tidy except for the closets.
There are so many things that I don't have a place for on paper
so they float in my bloodstream.
I am too much like a glass house.
Uncategorized thoughts are like stones.

I am often sweeping up the glass.

BURNING IN LAKE VOSTOK

The humiliation finally found where I live.
It finally broke through the protective covering.
It came in disguised as commitment.
It left the landscape torn and leaking.
It exposed what I had been protecting.

There is a familiar place where the earth is upside down.
The land is cold and hard.
The land is thick.
Millions of years of layers
Solidifying, growing, changing

Protecting
Hiding something pure...

(What they learned)
Under the ice is a jewel of a lake
Pure, expansive, and quiet.

We have burned to the core.
My humiliation has unearthed a sea of knowledge.
It might have told me I am strong.
Or that I am wise.
I am good
I am powerful
I am beautiful
But it didn't.
I have learned one thing in this lake:
I can't swim.
At the turn of the century
they thought the world would end
and we laughed.
(It didn't end)

The world did change to the degree that nothing will ever
    look the same to me again.

The January winds were relentless.

I am burning in this lake

I am my own house.

The walls have come up.

I have carried the walls of my old rooms into the brand new
    century.

I can't believe what I've done.

I am tight in places I shouldn't be.

Borderlines: A Horror Story in 7 Small Parts

Introduction

Spend a lifetime inventing broken characters

and don't ask why or how

when they end up in you like a thousand shards of glass

and splinters.

You miss the joke.

Spend a lifetime hiding from monsters and you blind
  yourself to the ones inside of you.

1.

First,

you are hollowed out.

But maybe not.

I'm already remembering it wrong.

Maybe, before that,

you're just *worn out*,

chased through the woods by a man, or something
  resembling a man,

wielding a rusted tool from the shed that you know will not

be quick nor painless.

Something that will hurt in a way you can't prepare for.

So you run and run and run,

on the ankle you just sprained in a divot.

If you hear that *snap*, it will be over faster.

The running, that is. Everything else will have just begun.

You listen and wait. The snapping is sticks, not bones.

Not yet.

But you run and run and run,

with the cramping in your side,

and lungs that feel like you've inhaled winter razors.

It feels like stabbing, you think but

You'd be so wrong.

You're about to find out.

You run and run and run,

with no sense of direction

other than

away.

But unlike the man with the rusted tool, you have not

trained for this.

As a child, you never thought,

one day...

When *I* was a child, I never thought I'd need to run.

I only knew I needed to hide,

so I became a ghost.

But I was not trained to run,

never ridden, never raced.

Breeds like me are broken in, but not in the fields,

not on the trails.

So if you're a breed like me,

you can only run so far before you have to stop.

And it's upon you now, which brings us back to the hollowing.

2.

The hollowing out of a person,

in this context,

is not the desired end result.

It's the kitchen counter full of pink fluids and glistening

bits on Thanksgiving.

It's filling and stringing up a pinata.

It's turning a canyon into a landfill.

It's the act of creating a void—which was inevitable when

you think about it—

and re-filling the cavity with even worse decay.

You are your own Pandora's Box.

Every ugly thing needs a home, and the space inside your
    head works nicely.

The space inside your chest...

even better.

A little further south, and disembowelment offers spatial

options that seem to defy physics.

All that loss,

and pain,

and malice...

you can fold it,

layer it,

coil it inside,

until you can barely tell it isn't the entrails you started with.

3.

So there you are,

strung up in the shed.

You can see the things that used to be inside you in a tub in

the corner.

Someone or some thing will eat them and they will be gone.

You mourn the loss of these things, because you don't

realize there is something else in you now,

growing,

evolving.

You think you are empty,

and this is how you will justify everything to come.

Choking Back the Devil

It was the loss.

It was grief.

It was someone you loved,

and because you loved them,

when it was time,

you made the decision.

And you wanted to run and run and run then,

but you were not trained for it.

So you stayed.

Because where will you go?

Loss finds everyone.

Even the ghosts,

and the really excellent hiders.

It is real when the light goes out in someone you love.

You feel it,

like an electric charge in the air,

in a storm.

There is a flash of terror in your head,

for yourself, and for them...

then

nothing.

You carry what's left of them home in a plastic bag with a
    hard handle.

Their clothing,

shoes,

glasses.

A necklace, maybe.

How can you even tell?

It all just looks like pieces of them.

Because it's just a container of entrails, of insides,

to be consumed, in time.

All of it will end up in a container. A coffin, an urn, that
    empty space in your chest.

And you wait and wait

to feel something again.

4.

Take in all the empathy,

all the sympathy while you can.

The well-wishes, the visitors, having your erratic behaviors
    excused and tolerated take it all.

Even though you know it's just going to seep into the void

and dissipate

the way enzymes break down,

you take it,

because before long,

there will be no more.

5.

Here's where the story changes.

No more tool sheds, no faceless men hunting you.

Now we are in the realm of demons.

Possession by an entity of no discernible origin.

No name.

It all looks normal, a normal setting, on any given normal day.

The storm has passed, and that means it's all right, right?

If you don't look anyone in the eye, no one will know.

At least for a while.

If you let it in and let it out as it pleases, and don't fight, it
    will come and go with little fanfare.

It is, of course, filling you with poison, consuming the
    poison, regurgitating

the poison, on and on forever, until you are nothing but a
    toxic canyon.

You keep the outside pretty, for desperate, selfish tourists.

They've come to see the sights.

Tequila sunrises and tear-stained sunsets.

Lies for miles and black-out skies you'll never remember,
    because your damaged brain never filmed it.

The thing swimming in your empty shell tells you to be glad.

Be glad you'll never know.

It's one of the two kind things it will ever do for you.

(The second kind thing comes later)

Like when the person who just violated you, gives you a

    tissue to dry your tears.

Thanks, you said.

Thanks.

6.

You're a different sort of ghost now.

Once,

you were quiet and harmless.

Just a shadow,

a memory,

a whisper,

A hider.

A spectral woman who weeps quietly in a child's bedroom,

or the child, itself,

taken too young.

It doesn't even know it should be angry.

But now you are different.

You know.

The thing that possessed you isn't slipping in and out so

    easily now.

It's tearing holes where there were none.

It's chewing through what's left of you.

It's biting at your feet and legs when you walk by the bed.

It's digging at you with a blunt, broken nail, rolling up strips
of skin like wood shavings.

It's slamming into you, full force, the second you close your eyes.

It slams out the same way,

a perpetual car crash.

You come home battered. You wake up bruised.

But there's no assailant.

All anyone can see is you.

You are a different sort of ghost,

haunting yourself until you cross the borderline and die a
second death.

7.

One step.

You only have to take this one step.

Maybe it's off a bridge, or maybe it's out the door.

It doesn't really matter—the outcome is going to be the same.

But you still believe there are greener pastures on the other side.

On the other side, you'll feel better.

The poison will drain.

The canyon will become a lake, filled with water,

cold and clear from some (in)eternal spring.

Then the demon, the entity that possessed and poisoned

you does the second kind thing—

It tells you what a stupid cunt you are for believing there
was ever a spring,

or a pasture,

or anything other than the pain you've been hiding from
your entire life.

And that's when houses start shaking, and walls start
bleeding, and screams start emanating from the cellars,
and you have to grab what's left of your family and the
pets and run and run and run like hell.

You start praying to a god you don't even believe in
anymore, all the while knowing that the scene unfolding
before you, threatening to destroy everything you ever
loved, was created by you.

Your creation.

You approached the Event Horizon.

You crossed the borderline.

And the real punch in the gut is

All that running you did—

When you never had to take more than one step.

Afterword

Beautiful Little Terrors:
Horror Poetry's Place in the Genre
(first published by Ladies of Horror Fiction)

I've had the honor and good fortune to be nominated this year for a Bram Stoker Superior Achievement in Poetry Award for a collection titled WITCHES, beautifully illustrated and designed by my collaborator Steven Archer.

The most common query, upon sharing the news, has been: There's such a thing as horror poetry?

I'm not surprised. In the "mainstream" world, it's been a very long time since people gathered in parlors to entertain one another with these dark, lyrical gems—my younger years as a goth teen hanging with friends in graveyards notwithstanding.

Once we've established that there is, indeed, such a thing as horror poetry, the next natural question would be: What purpose does it serve?

As with most art—far beneath the myriad large-scale impacts upon societies—I can only tell you how this particular medium serves me.

I've written two horror novels and a novella, and it felt like it took an eternity. I had histories and backstories for every character that never made it to the page. I researched, outlined, dreamed, and fretted over the details of their lives, and though I enjoyed it, that process eventually removed me from the fear and ugliness I was trying to convey. It became matter-of-fact and clinical after all those months, and all I really wanted was to be back in their dark world. In the end, I got there, but it was not a simple journey.

Poems—those brief moments of terror or pain—allow for that immersion. The horror novel may be the long, quiet walk down the hall that you know can't end well. The horror poem is the shrouded figure with bone-cutting shears rushing at you from behind.

Poetry is that nightmare that didn't make enough sense to tell a comprehensive story. It was just a brief, unsettling moment of pictures and feelings, your brain desperately trying to find patterns in chaos.

It is the challenge of simplifying trauma and fear, and manipulating it into a sweet-sounding rhyme or a piece no longer than a shopping list.

The horror novel may be hundreds of needles inserted into flesh over the course of days or weeks, but the poem—if done right—can be an ax right to the torso.

And what a power to wield. As a poet I want to entertain you but I also want to make you hurt. I want you to be uncomfortable. I want you to be afraid and unsettled. And I want to do it with the smallest, most unassuming tool possible.

For the horror poet, the possibilities of creativity and villainy are endless, because if you can scare someone with ten words, imagine what you could do with ten-thousand.

Choking Back the Devil

About the Author

Donna Lynch is a dark fiction writer and the co-founder—along with her husband, artist and musician Steven Archer—of the dark electro-rock band Ego Likeness (Metropolis Records). Her written works include *Isabel Burning*, *Red Horses*, *Driving Through the Desert*, *Ladies & Other Vicious Creatures*, *Daughters of Lilith*, and *In My Mouth*. Lynch's poetry collection *Witches* was nominated for a Bram Stoker Award. She and her husband live in Maryland.

www.ingramcontent.com/pod-product-compliance
Lightning Source LLC
LaVergne TN
LVHW041202080426
835511LV00006B/704